GRUEL

Gruel

Bunkong Tuon

The New York Quarterly Foundation, Inc.
New York, New York

NYQ Books™ is an imprint of The New York Quarterly Foundation, Inc.

The New York Quarterly Foundation, Inc.
P. O. Box 2015
Old Chelsea Station
New York, NY 10113

www.nyq.org

First Edition

Set in New Baskerville

Layout by Macaulay Glynn and Mickey Kellam

Cover Design by Mickey Kellam

Cover Photo: The author's parents' wedding (circa 1972). In the center are Chhoeun Thach (his father), Noerm Tuon (his mother), and to her left, Yoeum Preng (his grandmother).

Author Photo by Nicole M. Calandra

Library of Congress Control Number: 2015942607

ISBN: 978-1-63045-006-9

Gruel

Contents

III: I NEVER KNEW HOW TO THANK YOU

IV: WEST COAST

V. WHAT WE TALK ABOUT WHEN WE TALK ABOUT WRITING

VI: DAY WORK

VII: CAMBODIA

In Memory of Yoeum Preng

1929–2015

I: FAMILY PORTRAIT

The House of Many Voices

You can get lost if you pay attention
to the creaking in the sad murmurs
underneath the floorboard. I told my wife,
whatever you do, don't look over

your shoulder, or you will be snagged
by a ghost of rice paddies and water
buffalo, its heavy black hair still wet
from the mist of yesteryear, or a ghost

of the missing son, whose memory lives
in the furtive glances of uncles and aunts,
in the grandmother who refuses death.
There are many ghosts here. Listen,

I was caught by one of these ghosts
the other day, and I am telling you this,
passing it on to you, not in some spirit
of generosity, but so that I can be free.

Grandmother-Mother

I've been avoiding that dreaded phone call from home.
When we did talk, I made up excuses why I couldn't visit:
my first year at the school, teaching new classes,
publish or perish. You said you understood. The truth is,
I am afraid to find out the truth. I am afraid, afraid.

Grandmother, you are my closest connection to mother.
You were there when I was born, and took care of me when mother
died. When the Khmer Rouge fell, you told Father
now he had a new wife and with a new wife came children,
you were afraid I would become the unwanted one.
I wonder if you also told him this: I was what was left of your daughter.

You took me away from the father whom I know little about,
the one I invent and reshape in the stories and poems about our family.
With your surviving sons and daughters, you carried me on your back,
across the heavily-mined jungles of Cambodia to the UN camps,
scattered somewhere along the Thailand-Cambodia border.

I was six or seven at the time. I don't remember
how old exactly. Time confuses.
But I remember the swaying
                        the comforting
                                    the soothing rhythm

as you carried me on your back.
In Pol Pot's time, I was protected, sheltered, loved, always.
I was, indeed, a lucky child.

And now, that child you carried on your back across Cambodia's border,
on a boat crossing the Gulf of Thailand, through the Indonesia islands,
all the way to the doorstep of our Christian sponsor in Massachusetts,
it is that child's turn to carry you, Grandmother-Mother.

Reciting Alphabets

Srak-aw, srak-ah, srak-aek, srak-aye, srak-ouk, srak-o ...

I recited these sing-song syllables
as I stepped inside the revolving door,
walked up to the front desk,
hands sweating, voice shaking,
told the clerk about my appointment,
took the elevator to the ninth floor,
trembled in the hallway,
trembled in front of the door
when memories of you
gave me courage to knock
for a job interview that would take me
to Upstate New York, far from you.

Srak-aw, srak-ah, srak-aek, srak-aye, srak-ouk, srak-o ...

These were the Khmer vowels
I recited at Khao-I-Dang camp.
You and Grandmother sat
proudly as I struggled:

Srak-aw, srak-ah, srak-aek, srak-aye, srak-ouk, srak-o...

Years later in Long Beach, you grew sick.
And I, a young man living at home, grew tired
of your constant needs until Grandmother
reminded me of those nights at the camp
when I sang these vowels
and you looked on in quiet delight.

Srak-aw, srak-ah, srak-aek, srak-aye, srak-ouk, srak-o...

Here is your story, Grandfather.
You were the head monk at the local monastery,
the last bastion of our ancient civilization,

when the Khmer Rouge came to power
and made you this offer: take a wife
or face the executioner's blade.
All at once, you learned to be a husband,
a father to my uncles and aunts,
and a grandfather to me.
You accepted life's greatest
attachment, love, without fuss.

Srak-aw, srak-ah, srak-aek, srak-aye, srak-ouk, srak-o

This year, I returned to Long Beach
for a reading. As if called, I asked a friend
to drive me to Forest Lawn.
And this song I heard:

Srak-aw, srak-ah, srak-aek, srak-aye, srak-ouk, srak-o...

So far away, yet so familiar on my tongue,
like lime, *prahouk*, and green chilis,
like incense, *pali*, and orange robes.
I knelt before your headstone,
placing flowers of gratitude.

Photograph of My Mother on Her Wedding Day

In the black-and-white wedding photograph
you stand next to your husband—
confident, smiling, looking directly
into the camera, jewels glittering.
That necklace Grandmother borrowed
from the landowner whose house stood
between the fish market and noodle shops,
where the train snaked alongside the marketplace,
where is it now?

This must be before 1975, before strange cravings,
when your sister, barely a teenager, barefoot
and tired, waded through muddy rice fields,
on thin, stilted legs, searching for eels,
and you, rib-cage thin, pale,
skin about to burst, eyes bulging,
cold, always cold, waiting for her
to bring back lizards, snakes, crickets, eels;
before Buddhist monks chanting prayers
on our house's veranda, and me
crying under the tamarind tree,
thinking how those monks were so rude,
bothering your sleep.

Thirty years later, my fingers trace the worn-out texture,
the duct tape wrapping the photograph's torn corners,
and I am paralyzed.
You smile so brilliantly
that even your sisters,
who now have children of their own,
would blush at your boldness.

Mother, I am about to marry.
I wish we had a chance to talk.
I have no memory of you;
even a fragment of you angry, screaming

at something I did, pulling a nearby branch,
would help me imagine
what you would say to me now.

Lies I Told about Father

I believed I had the power to revive you,
to sit you up in the family's pigsty,
drunk off your ass, smiling at nothingness,
the late morning light shining on your face.
With a son's quiet adoration, I chiseled you:
a gangster from the East, a *Khmer Krom*
whose blood cried out Khmer characters (not Vietnamese),
who, guided by fate, found himself in the West
and married mother for her virtue and beauty.

In these poems you drink because, well, real men
drink, curse, and sleep around (the cursing
and sleeping around, you didn't do, of course,
because of your love and respect for Mother).
I was an aspiring writer then,
renting a tiny studio on Ocean Boulevard
in Long Beach, following in the drunken
bouts of Charles Bukowski, buying cheap wine,
imitating free verse,
waking up to the stench of sour vomit.
Of course, this life did not last long.
I can't hold liquor, let alone women.
I have always been a reader,
safe behind words, punctuation, and sentences,
between the pages, where I can conquer
an entire nation or seduce women with my long dash—.

Now, I am engaged to a kind, generous person.
Mother would approve of her.
I am returning to you once again,
not for approval, just to talk,
son to father, but it dawns on me:
I am without you.

First Snow

We huddled
behind the back door
of our sponsor's house.

My uncle, the bravest
because he spoke a little English,
went out.

My grandmother, aunts,
and I watched him
through the kitchen window.

He bent down, reached for
the whiteness of this new world,
and put some in his mouth.

He looked back at us and smiled,
"We can make snow cones with this!"

America, the miraculous, our savior,
you were the land of dreams then.

Fishing for *Trey Platoo*

You might have seen them
fishing on the shores of the Cape Cod Canal:

My uncle in his fisherman's hat
pulling in a one-foot *scup*, my aunt in her pajama-like

pants walking backward up the bike path,
snapping a line that's gotten stuck between the rocks,

my other aunt reeling in a sea bass,
her husband by her side directing.

Bikers, joggers, teenagers and their dates,
families with their children look curiously on.

Or maybe you have seen them
lining up all three sides of a pier in Salem,

their wrists jerking in a language
that bewitches the squids below.

They are not the only ones.
Other Cambodians and Vietnamese, once enemies,

fish side by side on the same American pier.
Other immigrants, Chinese, Spanish, Portuguese

speaking languages I can't understand, come together
on this spot: sacred rods in hands, beckoning the squid.

Or maybe you have seen them
under a bridge fishing the Providence River,

looking for *trey platoo*, a type of mackerel
they used to eat in the refugee camps in Thailand.

Sometimes, my aunts and uncles run into an old friend
from those long ago days. They talk about the lack

of food, of sneaking out at night to fish, and of running,
always running, from the Thai police.

They exchange phone numbers, share fishing secrets,
and set up a time and place where they'll fish together again.

When they get home, my aunts gut the fish,
clean them, fry them, and put them in a boiling stew

of galangal, lemongrass, and kaffir leaves.
My uncles and aunts sit in a circle on the floor,

eat, and tell stories of how this fish got away
or how one of them got caught by the Thai police.

No matter how hard they try, they can never understand
why my cousin and I ever bother with fishing—

Why we catch and release food, as if it's some sport.

Where Uncle Dreams

Ten years ago, the city dreamed
a new beginning for itself, cleaning up
the streets and alleyways,
where if you missed a turn, you found yourself
in a neighborhood where only Spanish was spoken,
and before that, Italian and Yiddish
were heard in delis and corner shops.
The city's dream swept up
my uncle's video store, indifferent
to the friendships he built as he swept the front,
shelved empty sleeves, rewound videotapes,
answered the phone, and greeted everyone
with, "Hello. Thank you for your business."
He decided not to fight, he said,
because America brought us here.
We should be grateful for that,
no matter what happened now.
I didn't mention Nixon and Kissinger
bombing our countryside in '69.

Now at home, he cares for his ailing mother,
who hears little English and speaks Khmer,
and his grandchildren, who understand Khmer
but speak only English. Whenever I visit,
my uncle likes to show my wife and me
home videos of relatives visiting temples,
waterfalls, and ancient ruins,
attending weddings, funerals, and *Pchum Ben*,
praying to ancestors, burning incense,
making offerings to hungry ghosts.
To appease his own ghosts, he sent money
earned from the sweat of a thirteen-hour shift
and the fear of robbery, fear held at bay
by beliefs in fate, karma, and Buddha.

Recently, my uncle has been talking
about living out his days in Cambodia.
He sends whatever savings to his cousins
for a house they are building in Battambang.
He shows us email pictures of the house.
A two-story colonial house, its columns
sturdy and proud: a promise.
He stops to apologize to my wife
for his poor English and asks me to translate.
Then he turns to the four Apsara statues behind him,
each pair guarding one side of the large television.
He tells us, "Each celestial creature is dancing
her cosmic dance. Look how unique is her face,
how each smile brings joy and happiness."
I ask how much he spent on those things.
"Four thousand dollars," he says.
I study them searching those almond-shaped
Cambodian eyes for the clouds and mist,
traces of their divine nature.

Literary Success

(for Tony)

I called the uncle whom I love
and told him that the Long Beach reading
went well: people were moved.
He asked, did you get paid?
I said, no, it's not that kind of success.
People now know our stories.
I told him about this poet, Tony Gloeggler,
who said that he liked my poems.
Now, Tony's editor wanted
to see my manuscript. That's like,
I tried to explain, winning the lottery.
Well, he said, where is this is editor from?
New York City, I said. Good, he said,
and asked, how long is this book going to be?
I hope it'll be at least 200 pages long.

Fishing with My Cousin

At Swain's Pond, catching crappies all afternoon.
On the ground a plastic container of what's left
of a dozen Canadian night crawlers.
A spoken silence connects us.
It's mid-August, probably our last fishing
run before school starts.
The sun hot on our faces, the water still,
the leaves whisper. Those crappies—
they bite, they pull, they turn, they twist
this way and that, blue flashing, tail lashing,
making waves over a half-torn worm,
which by some miracle is still alive, twirling
endlessly in its brownness on a hook.

Under the Tamarind Tree

The child sits on the lap
of his aunt, under the old tamarind tree
outside the family home.

The tree stands still, quiet,
indifferent. The house sways
on stilts.

Monks in saffron robes,
and nuns with shaved heads,
lips darkened with betel-nut stain,

sit chanting prayers
for the child's mother.

Incense perfumes the hot dry air.

There emerges a strange familiar song
between the child and his aunt that day—
a distant one, melodic but harsh,
as if the strings are drawn too tight—

Each time the child hears prayers
coming from the house, he cries;
each time he cries, the aunt, a girl herself,
pinches the boy's thigh.

II: EAST COAST

Snow Day

Silent as night
the morning snow covered
the school, the playground.
A ghost town in this city near the beach.
But no one told this refugee child
about such a day. No one said
to turn on the TV. No one called.

He walked in the white field
looking up to the sky, raising his hands,
letting his brown body fall backward
into the white landscape.
His eyes closed,
each flake gently caressing
his cheeks.

Our Neighborhood in Revere, MA
(circa 1984 and 2008)

Listen, you have seen it before
in countless movies and TV shows.
No matter which city it is,
the markers are the same:

The sneakers on telephone wires,
the cracked sidewalks, the potholes
you try so hard to avoid
you almost hit the double-parked cars,
the graffiti on street signs and public buildings,
the apartment complex and family houses slumped
so close together that you can smell
your neighbor's fried pork with rice,
where you can taste the lemongrass, fish sauce,
red chilies, and brown golden garlic,
as if your grandmother is cooking next door.
Houses where English is not spoken,
and the first image greeting you might not be Christ,
where you need to lift up the reservoir's lid and pull
the string to flush the toilet,
where young men hang out on the front porch
with broken windows and no future.
An air conditioner sits on the brown grass.
A mother walks down the sidewalk,
some of her children running ahead of her,
a baby in only a diaper,
cradled to her chest.

You have seen it on the local news.
A young reporter staring wide-eyed
speaking with anxiety and concern
about a shooting that claimed the lives
of young bystanders, about a drug bust
where police found some untold
amount of coke, and you're shaking

your head, wondering what the world
has come to, now that these foreigners
are ruining our America.

I was in the old neighborhood the other day
with my fiancée. Fresh from graduate school
studying postcolonial literature and theory
we went there to pick up some curry.
I scanned, trying to get a sense of the scene,
making sure the car doors are locked.
The streets, the smells, the sights reminded
me of the old days, the markers were all there,
but the people that I knew were gone.
Now there were Middle Easterners.
I guess the United States was no longer at war
with Southeast Asia.

Our Secret

Back in the day, we must have looked really strange
to onlookers. When the light changed, we crossed
the street, a caravan of two—an old lady
pushing a cart filled with empty soda cans
and beer bottles, followed aimlessly by a thin boy,
about eight or nine years old, with a protruding stomach
and a clear plastic bag filled with more cans and bottles.
On those summer days, we scavenged the trash
cans along the shoreline of Revere Beach,
where the Americans sunbathed in their scanty
swimwear, and, to our amazement, tried
to get a sun tan, trying to brown their skin like ours,
trying to look like farmers from the countryside.

We should have told them our secret:
Walk in the sun all day
collecting empty bottles and cans;
Walk, don't drive, to a nearby liquor store,
and wait in line (with shame on your face
and dark syrup clinging to your fingers)
as the cashier lady counts the bottles and cans,
as disgruntled beachgoers wait in line behind us.
We never made enough money
to justify the shame I felt, but Grandmother
was proud to take home the $15.75.

Halloween, 1985

The saliva on your face
(for all the world to see!).

A lifetime of desire, a daily prayer
for death, a return to the beginning,
a place of warmth and affection,
a desire to be with Mother.

An Elegy for a Fellow Cambodian

The reason Vannark got into that fight
      was because Rob had called him a dog-eater.

Dancing Fu Manchu Master

One day, walking home
by myself, a blue plastic backpack slung
over my shoulders, a Christmas gift
from our sponsor, I noticed three boys
watching me from the convenience store
down the corner near an apartment complex.
The leader, a short, red-haired, chubby kid,
stepped out of the shadow, and called out,
"Ching Chong, are you from Hong Kong?"
I quickened my pace pretending
to hear my Grandmother calling me.
"Hey, can you help me with my math homework?"
They burst out laughing.
Seeing me walk firmly away, they slurred out
a slew of hurtful words.
"Why don't you go back to China?"
"Do you eat dogs where you come from?"
"You use grass and leaves to wipe your ass, right?"
"Do you know Kung Fu?"

With this last question saliva,
warm and gooey, hit my neck.
I closed my eyes, counted my steps,
mindful of my breath, my heart slowed.
I jumped and turned,
thirty feet straight into the air,
took out my sword, with a flick
of the wrist, saw heads roll,
tumbling away down the sidewalk,
bodies slumped behind:
red blossoming concrete.

Trained in the mysterious arts
of Dr. Fu Manchu, I made myself
disappear before the police arrived.

Why I Chose Literature

It was Mr. Henry
who told me to stand up
when I received the highest
grade on an algebra test.
He lectured to the class
about how I had escaped war,
poverty, and hunger,
about how I worked hard
and achieved success.

The lesson was supposed
to embarrass my classmates
into working hard, but I'm afraid
it only encouraged them
to punch my head
even harder, after school.

Losing One's Name

It began with loss:
a loss of homeland, of ancestors,
a loss of stories, of history.
With loss came death,
or a desire for it,
the annihilation of pain,
but death was not possible,
so you settled for invisibility,
disappeared into the whiteness,
became an absence,
desired to escape the brownness
that was always yours,
a brownness that didn't exist before.
The name given by friends
because yours was hard to pronounce,
you didn't mind it. One
syllable was easier to say,
culled from Dr. Seuss, a name
like any other name in school,
on television, in this new world:
Sam or Bunkong,
not much competition really.

Ollieing over Obstacles

All you have is this 8 X 30 board
that protects flesh from concrete,
keeps anger from consuming.

No matter the hill, you must control
this Caballero dragon,
keep it firmly under your feet,
or else, a twisted ankle, a bloodied shin,

A nice concussion. Most times
the blood is spilled by accident,
other times you need to make sure
this hurt is of your own making.

Saturday Morning in Malden, MA (1986)

Saturday morning
grocery shopping at the only Asian
market in the city;
putting back fish sauce and soy sauce,
picking up milk, bread, and cereal,
I told Grandma to be quiet—

Because Stephanie and her mother were there too.

Those Were the Days

(for Sophetra)

On those long summer days
we bombed down Truman Drive
on our GT and Mongoose bikes,
crossed Broadway/Route 99,
passed the bowling alley where
I ditched classes to play Ms. Pacman,
and rode up a small hill,
where Mt. Hood sat to our right—

There, we entered our emerald forest,
of shade and cool wind,
our reflectors flickering sunlight.
We popped wheelies, bunny hopped
over ditches and sewer covers,
and leaned our bikes to the side
for those sharp blind turns, as if
we were on those Kawasaki Ninjas,
not thinking whether the next turn
would yield a suburban mother
in her station wagon
or a truck tunneling its way
to the plant across the highway.

No matter how hard we tempted
fate, we never got hurt,
as if someone was watching over us,
as if our time hadn't come yet,
as the suffering of the adult world
waited patiently for us to enjoy
the pure joy of being young.

One day, a friend showed up
with a Mike McGill skateboard,
the one with a serpent wrapping
around a skull with red eyes.

It was obvious to us, then,
that we each needed one.
I got myself a used Tony Hawk.

We didn't have to go far.
As soon as we left the door,
the world was our playground.
We did slappies and board slides
on curbs in our neighborhood.
We learned to ollie over curbs,
train tracks, and, later, stairs.
At night, we grinded the hell
out of the curb at the local bank.

Sparks flew. The night lit up,
as metal grinded against metal,
with the faint scent of burnt skin.
Our young bodies smashed
against pavement, our knees bloodied,
Our hands on the ground
in some midnight prayer.

Those were the days,
with Jolt Cola and beef jerky
in my stomach, I skated past the setting sun,
with the world asleep,
and the thing that could contain
the rage inside was that board.

Those were the days
when we skated in suburban malls,
where we had our own language,
like "gnarly," "awesome," and "totally rad,"
to lay claim to everything we did,
and as for the rest of the world,
we simply didn't care.

Rhonda Said

Her mother was a stripper
at the local club. At night,
we heard Mrs. Gilroy staggered
up the stairs, yelling at some guy
she was seeing that week.
We heard heels clomping
above us, something crashed,
and Mrs. Gilroy laughing.
Then things got quiet
until the bed began to squeak.
On weekends, Mrs. Gilroy stood
on the patio, cigarette in hand,
staring in disgust at us refugee
kids playing in the backyard.
We looked up. Her radio blasting,
"You Shook Me All Night Long."

One day after school Rhonda
said her mother was at work.
So I climbed up those stairs.
We sat on the stained yellow
couch that reeked of cigarettes
and tuna fish watching *As
The World Turns*
when Rhonda got up,
led me to the bedroom,
her hand tiny and warm.
She unbuttoned my fly
and pulled down my jeans.
She studied it, and said
that this was what they did
in the magazines left by
her mother's boyfriends.
I clutched the bed post.

That summer, Rhonda
and her mother moved
to somewhere in Texas,
where she learned
about Vietnam and Long
Duk Dong, where she started
to spit out her mother's
words at the Vietnamese
refugees who began
showing up everywhere,
on the street, in supermarkets,
in the fishing village
where Rhonda's stepfather
was from, whose faces
looked like my own.

Lessons

(for my cousins)

When we were younger, I made
my cousins fight each other in the dark.
We were in the basement room
my uncle had fixed up for guests.
I helped them put layers of socks
on their fists, told them to stay
in their little corner of the room.
They were six to nine years old.
I was about fourteen: thin,
the smallest kid in high school.
Grandma was upstairs taking
care of the little ones.
Their parents were at work
in New Hampshire factories,
Maine lumber companies.
Using the toughest voice
I could muster, "I'm going to count
to ten and shut off the light.
See where each other is now.
Imagine where your opponents will be
Then go get them."
Before reaching ten, I turned off the light,
screamed, "Go!"
A minute later, I heard bodies being tagged,
crashing into each other and falling.
They were yelling, screaming,
groaning in that dark room.
Three minutes into the melee, I turned
on the light, "Enough. Stop!"
Someone was injured. I picked him up,
put my hands on his shoulders,
and said, "This is a crazy, mean, cruel world,
you must have tough skin to survive it.
Now stop crying and get ready for round two."

That summer, this same cousin was learning
to ride a bike. I walked alongside him
as he pedaled away from our home.
As soon as we couldn't be seen
by adults, I took a vice grip
from my jacket, loosened
the training wheel. "This is
the only way you will learn
to ride. You have to trust me."
I held the bike firmly, one hand
on the handlebar, the other gently
on his back. I ran with him
as he pedaled and with all the forces
in my heart, I pushed.
My cousin held on for five seconds
before he began leaning to the left,
crashing against a white picket fence.
I ran to him as he got up.
His shin was busted, skin torn,
blood trickled. I said, "Get up now.
You can do it. I believe in you.
You have to get up and try again.
Don't you see? I'm trying to toughen
you up! Get up. Stop crying, please."

Most of my cousins are now married,
some of them have children of their own.
I visited one of them the other day,
the one who cried for her mother
whenever we played the boxing game.
Her third child, a baby girl, sleeps
in my arms. I sit still on the couch
not wanting to disturb perfection.
Her skin soft, smooth, so new.
I tear up quietly in the living room.

Bad Day

One time, while doing a wheelie,
a golf ball flew over the trees
and hit the back of my shoulder,
leaving a dark purple bruise
the following day.
The golfers laughed.
I gave them the finger
and rode away.

Later that day,
while fishing at Swain's Pond,
the earth trembled,
the sky cried.
Water poured down
hard over my head.

Not a single bite
all afternoon.

Remembering

Nothing is wasted, not the hurtful words
when you were pushed and cornered,
warm spit on your cold cheeks,
an afterschool assault in the playground
because you were different and alone,
because the language was too new to fight back,
because the colorful church clothes you wore
were in fashion a decade ago.
The spitting stopped in high school,
but there was Joey who tried to burn you
with a cigarette lighter at the bus stop.
His pale lips quivered with excitement
as the blue light came close to your face.
Then there was the opposite sex,
dating, formal dances, the prom—
all of it, lethal to a child without parents,
driven by a question his uncles and aunts
couldn't answer: what did we do
to make them hate us so much?
Memorizing algebraic equations,
reading Shakespeare and Chaucer,
learning about the American Revolution,
didn't help. You went inward;
then the slipping of grades, the loss
of interest in everything, and an age-old
weariness that no child should carry.

What the Buddha Taught

Life, friend, is suffering.
When we attach ourselves
to the material, the physical,
which is always changing,
we cause our own suffering.

Let's look at it another way.

If life is one big change and nothing
is permanent, including suffering,
everything then is a gift,
a promise of potentiality,
the self expanding
in quiet infinite space.

That, friend, is happiness.

III: I NEVER KNEW HOW TO THANK YOU

Dead Tongue

I never knew how to thank you.
The words don't sound right.

My tongue has been cut
to fit the meter of another world.

The words bounce off walls,
deflated, a dead poem.

Calling Home

My cousin left me this message:
"Grandmother fell in the bathroom
and hit her head against the sink.
There's a small gash over her right eye."

I call home, and my uncle answers.
"No need to worry. You can't talk to her.
She's sleeping now. How's work?
When will you be up for that review?"

Breakfast with Grandmother

Her maroon beanie, a Christmas gift
from one of her grandchildren,
rests snuggly on her shaved head,
a stained bib around her neck.
The pills, crushed in a spoon,
sprinkle the murky gruel.
The water must be heated
to the right temperature, somewhere
between hot and not warm enough.
She cries each time one of us leaves
and is surprised when we return.

I sit at the table trying
not to stare at the cut near her temple,
watching her eat her breakfast,
to let her know that I am here
for her
when suddenly she screams in pain.

Afterward, she sobs quietly,
starring into the gruel
of Jasmine rice, chicken broth,
and now, tear and mucus.

Dining in Chinatown

My twenty-eight-year-old cousin says,
before putting a piece of sesame beef into his mouth,
"She can't be lonely. She has everyone by her side,
her children, grandchildren, and great-grandchildren."
He pours chili oil over black and pepper squid,
and continues, "Whatever she needs, we get for her.
Food, medicine. She has Elder Uncle who sleeps
in her room to make sure all her needs are met.
Unlike some of her friends whose children
are all over the States, she's lucky to have us around."

I watch, fascinated by his ability to take in all that food.
Maybe he's making up for all that lost time
in the refugee camp. "And that damaged nerve of hers,
her pain stops whenever you're around. It's psychosomatic,
or something like that. I don't know. You're the Ph.D."

Exile

From the couch she watches
her great-grandchildren chase
each other down the hallway.

Commanded by the eldest,
they are Power Rangers battling
some evil robot.

A smile flickers.
Memory lit, before it disappears
into darkness again.

My Four-Year-Old Niece's Birthday

I sit with the adults around the dining room.
Grandmother is having her lunch of
finely crushed rice powdered
with her daily medicine.

"She's fine. The doctor says
she needs to exercise."

"I try to get her to move around.
She walks a couple times
between here and the living room,
then sits on the couch,
and seconds later, she'll be snoring."

"She sleeps too much during the day.
At night, she keeps all of us up talking
about her husband, her young brother,
our missing brother,
and your mother."

"I get goose bumps sometimes,
listening to her talk like that."

"Doesn't she want to go to the temple anymore?
She has friends there and the monks really like her.
Didn't they come to bless her in August?"

"Her friends are old too. Grandma Jeat passed
away last month from cancer.
She was sixty three. Grandma is eighty four."

"Don't let her know."

"She needs to get out of the house
and be with people her own age. I see her sitting by

herself in the living room, watching the kids
run amok and yelling at them to speak Khmer."

"She's out of breath just walking
from here to the bathroom. Besides, it's getting cold outside.
She can't handle the weather that well now."

"When is her next doctor's visit? I'd like to go
with you, Uncle."

Staring at each of our faces,
Grandmother speaks in clear, measured Khmer:
"Why is everyone speaking English?
You think I don't know that you're talking about me?
'Doctor.' 'Hospital.' '*Yiey* Jeat.'
I'm no dummy. "

A Lesson

I tell myself.
There must be a lesson
in old age.
As the body withers,
truth appears.
It's wishful thinking,
but it's good
to think of hope
and renewal
in something beyond
our control.

But, seriously,
how long can we
ask this
of our elders?
How long can we
ask this
of ourselves?

Thanksgiving Farewell

Grandma is holding my wife's hand:

Take care of each other.
He doesn't have any parents.
I've taken care of him
since his mother passed
away under Pol Pot.

Grandma sobs and turns to me:
Tell her. Speak for me.

She places my hand on top of my wife's:
You. He. Take care.

Seeing our stunned faces, she repeats.
You. He. Take care. OK?

I give her a hug and say in Khmer:

There's no need to cry, *Lok-Yiey*.
We'll be back around Christmas.

Breathing In

Waiting for the broth to boil,
so that I can drop in the noodles

That Grandma used to make,

I imagine that phone call
from home,

The kind you see in the movies,
where a couple is awakened,

Two in the morning,
fumbling in a darkness

That will never leave.

I breathe in
to become part of you.

IV: WEST COAST

American Dream
Cambodian Style

My aunt screamed
and burrowed her face
into her hands. She sprang up
from the couch and bolted
for the bedroom. I knocked
on the door, "They are here
to help." She cried, "It's her.
She's brought her black friend
this time to finish the job."
I apologized to the detectives.
We went out to the courtyard
and watched the children
play in the swimming pool.

Back in the apartment, I found
my aunt sitting in the dark
next to the phone. She asked,
"What took you so long?
I was going to call the police.
I don't know what I'd say
to Grandma if they kidnapped you."
I asked, "Didn't you see their badges?"
"But they can make copies of those.
These days, you can't trust anyone,
especially those people."
I looked out the window
and saw a kid fly
from the balcony head first
into the shimmering blue water,
his friends laughing as if crying.

I remembered eight years ago
we were driving across the States.
My aunt and uncle took turns driving.
Sinn Sisamouth was singing

from the tape deck. I had just dropped
out of community college and had nothing
better to do. They were pursuing
the Cambodian version of the American
Dream: own a donut shop, make money,
send their kids to college.
My uncle reached out and wrapped
his right arm around his wife
as we headed west where the sun set.

Loneliness

Crying
on the park bench
I
saw a family
of squirrels
playing.

Renting a Room on Myrtle Avenue in Long Beach

Forest Lawn is the cleanest
place I have ever known.

I wish my yard was as big and clean
as this cemetery's lawn.

I wish we had flowers and memories.

Most of all, I wish my neighbors were
as peaceful and quiet as those occupants.

The Customer

When she walked through
the door, she had my skin
and a white Nirvana t-shirt

Of that American baby
in chlorine water chasing
that American dollar bill.

Glancing at the menu
she ordered in perfect English
a Caesar salad with Perrier.

The owner began making the salad
while his wife walked to the cooler
and opened its glass door.

The customer cried in Khmer
when she saw the plastic
bottle of water.

"Sorry, Sir,
that all we have right now.
No Perrier, Sir."

The customer hesitated,
then smiling, said, "Never mind.
Keep the change." And walked out.

The owner turned to me,
"You know, they are worse
than the real customers."

How Everything Changed

I was a college dropout working
in Southern California, scrubbing,
washing, mopping, emptying trash cans
of private homes, synagogues, local
schools, and offices in the L.B. shipyard,
nothing back breaking, just losing
a couple of hours of sleep each night.
One morning, out of boredom, I decided
to visit the local library, the kind where
old ladies push steel book carts
past little children playing, mothers gossiping,
the kind where you can disappear
quietly into the corner.
It was in one such corner, hidden away
from the sights and sounds of suburban
mothers and their children, where I
picked a random book off the shelf:
a book of poems by that drunken
old man, a book filled with social misfits
and outcasts, drunks and prostitutes,
barflies, cockroaches, and vomit;
at that moment, I felt my first breath.
I was gasping for air.
I felt my own sweet suffering in others.
Loneliness was extinguished,
and compassion bloomed in my chest.
I am telling you this, so that you know
in the worst storm of your life this mad love
can hit you, smashing you into a billion pieces,
connecting you with everyone and everything.

literary support

Uncle opened my bedroom door
found me shirtless on my bed
with Bukowski's *Septuagenarian Stew*
& slammed the door
in contempt
as if he had just caught me masturbating.

Driving from the Recycling Center

With eight dollars and fifty cents,
I hear my stomach growling:
A burger with fries and drinks
under five bucks, with a little change
for a microwave apple pie.
Burger King's around the corner.

Then I remember yesterday's trip
to Acres of Books:
A Vintage Contemporaries
of Carver's "Fires" was
$7.95, excluding tax.

A Whitman Reader went for $5.99.

"Fires" might go over the limit.
Whitman winks from the corner of his eye.

My stomach grabs a hold of the wheel,
hands shaking. But Whitman begins to sing:
"I loafe and invite my Soul;
I lean and loafe at my ease,
observing a spear of summer grass."

My car starts to sway to Whitman's songs
when someone in another lane honks,
"Hey, buddy, watch where you're going!"

Night Vision

(For Jordan Smith)

The moon cools
the desert highways.
The television lights
flicker off. Stars dangle
from the evening sky,
disturbed by the pounding
of the writer's keyboard.

Love

I woke up.

Grandma was
tailgating Grandpa
with a bucket.

Thundering Farts.
Pee soaked the sarong.
The stench mixed
with the humid air.

I got out of bed
and opened the windows,
sharing with our friendly
gang-infested neighborhood.
We were tired of him then.

When morning came
I brought him breakfast
of chicken soup and milk
with the doctor's pills
and a kiss on his forehead.

V. WHAT WE TALK ABOUT WHEN WE TALK ABOUT WRITING

The Atheist's Prayer

(for Clint)

I
forsake
God
because he
is
too difficult.

Writing

Blood blooms in red
velvet. The child, fascinated
with his wound, picks the scab,
web-like, brown, a foreign organism,
a small ugly planet on his knees.

Breathing Out

Life begins and ends
                with breath.
The first is quick,
short, filled with water.

The last one long, deliberately
measured, full of reflection.

Somewhere in between,
when you're gasping
                     for air,
keeping grace and dignity
is what counts.

What We Talk about When We Talk about Writing

1.
You are a good writer, he says.
They will publish your work, easily,
Because you write about being a minority.
You know, we suffer too.
We Irish are the Blacks of Europe.

You are a good writer, he says,
But you are no Hemingway, no Will Oldham.
You are no Hunter S. Thompson.
You will be known as "an ethnic writer."
It's your ticket to fame. And why, he asks,
Do you always bring up race when we talk?

Speaking of Bonnie Prince, there's a reading this evening.
You should check it out, he tells me.
My MFA buddies are doing some crazy shit.
Brad, you've seen him before, that dude
Who walks around campus in cowboy boots and hat?
He will be reading poetry and chugging Jim Beam.

And Gwen, his girlfriend, will sing her poems
With Brad accompanying her on guitar.
You should come.
You might learn a thing or two
About literature.

2.
You shouldn't write about women that way, she says.
Hemingway is long dead. Besides, you're an Asian-American.
You should write about things that matter:
Like race, gender, class, and power.

We are sitting in a Northampton coffee shop.
She talks between sips of latte
About her boyfriend, a hip-hop artist
Who slams poetry in Boston with his band.

She's the daughter of doctors,
I come from a long line of farmers.
She's a young professor at one of the local colleges,
I am a graduate student at the University.

She's telling me about Said and Spivak;
I'm told that I should read Marx and Gramsci—
I should attend conferences more often,
I should meet people, network, you know.

It's all performance, she says. Even gender
Is performance. Read Judith Butler. You should try—
Writing and publishing articles in scholarly journals.

I am sitting in this coffee shop in Northampton, MA,
With this beautiful, intelligent woman,
When suddenly, I had a bowel movement.

VI: DAY WORK

Fishing on Canandaigua Lake

In the evening breeze
he sits,
legs dangling
from a wooden plank.
A white planet
floats ten feet away.
Guided by silence
he waits.

Then slowly
voices rise
from the shimmering water,
from the whispering leaves,
to the misty air
toward the pink horizon.

His mind opens:
still breath, thought
crystal.

For Nicole

(After Carver's "For Tess")

My wife and I like to take walks
on the bike path along the Mohawk;
it is our dinner and a movie, our dancing
and drinking. Somehow, the dancing gene
was never passed down to me, and the drinking
I tried many times before, just bored me.
On these walks we talk about the struggle
of writing a line in a poem, a conference paper
in Chicago, an email to a student;
then the rest pours out, like her uncle who left
graduate school because he didn't like what he saw,
the lying and backstabbing, the pettiness of it all,
and that she needs to get the doctorate,
and I tell her about my grandfather's death,
how a twenty-year old kid sitting in a car wept
to some god-awful Britney Spears song.
There is silence between us.
I look to see that no one is in sight,
then steal a kiss on her warm cheek,
a peck, something light and quick—
the blurring sound of a hummingbird.

Healing

(For David Kaczynski)

Crystals flow
in perfect purity
with such force
bending this way
and that, against, around,
and above, smoothing edges
of mossy rocks, gently
and violently, rushing
into the brook's foamy mouth.

If you listen carefully, David,
you'll hear the distant song
of our births, reminding us
where we came from
and how to live harmoniously
with the enemies in our heart.
And if you continue sitting still
and listen with your whole being,
you can feel the here & now,
eternity within reach,
the Dharma in us.

Living in the Hyphen

Thanksgiving.
Driving home from school with a migraine
I pulled over and vomited on the side of Route 2.
I had been working on an article exploring
the implications of Bhabha's third space, searching
for a theory of an authentic hyphenated, diasporic, transnational,
(or was it post-national?) transglobal Asian-American identity.

When I arrived at my family's home,
my fifteen-year old cousin Thearith, the tallest
in our extended family, was having dinner.
Born in the States, he greeted me in his perfect
Bostonian accent. I watched him attack his steak.

On the table, with the dishes
of rice and steak, were two plates:
One contained a Khmer dipping sauce,
made of *prahouk*, lime juice, lemongrass,
grilled peppers, garlic, and Thai chilies;
the other, A1 Steak sauce
from the local Stop & Shop.

"Thearith, why do you have two sauces for your steak?"

"Well, when I get bored with one sauce, I go for the other.
It's all good, bro."

Work-Related Trauma

It's 4:30 a.m. The wife's asleep.
With your second cup of coffee
(black this time), staring blankly
at the computer screen, the birds chirping,
a lone car crawling by your window—
you're working on an article, looking
for an angle that adds something new
to an already existing body of work.
The alarm goes off, and it's 15
minutes before your first class, as you dash
off to campus, only to find a classroom
of unfamiliar faces, the department chair
looking amused in the back.
You realize only too late that you forget
your lesson plan and everyone's waiting
for you to say something—

Then it hits you:
you must still be in bed.
Any time now, you will wake up.
Any time now, the alarm will go off.
Any time now. . . *oh God, please.*

At the Nursery

Just the other day, I had an urge to buy a tomato plant.
Like hunger, stomach empty, fingers shaking,
this urge came without warning, without beginning,
no origin that I can detect, just *sensations,*
the quivering desire to plant, use my hands
to dig into the dark soil, moistened with dew,
smell the plant's green scent, care, protect,
love, and watch its flowers grow and bear fruit.
So I drove with my heart on the wheel
to a farm stand on the side of a road,
walked around, whistling between aisles
of flowers and veggies, until the counter girl
was free. I went up to her and asked,
"Do you sell tomato plants here?"
She answered with amusement and sadness,
"We are no longer selling those.
It's late in the season, and if you are starting now,
nothing will grow.
You might have a few green tomatoes,
and then the cold will come and wither them."
With such news, I drove home, regret in my stomach,
knowing that I will have to face the coming winter alone.

3:45 AM

(After Kharms's "Plummeting Old Women")

My wife was sleeping ever so quietly
when I heard a tapping, quite obtrusively
yet somehow familiar, outside our window.
I got up to look and saw no one.
I went back to bed, when suddenly
the tapping returned—now, a playful
tap, tap, tap, a beckoning call,
maybe to a late-night caroling,
or to early morning prayer—
who knows?

When I reached the window,
again I saw no one.
My wife called for me to return to bed,
when that tapping returned,
the same harried tap, tap, tap.
I quickly stuck my head out
and saw Danill Kharms
and Alexander Vvedensky,
my old Russian hooligans from high school,
now in clown outfits, sticking their tongues out,
giggling like schoolgirls—

Go back to bed and be with your wife, they say.

What Was That?

Morning, the heater crackles. Hot steam rises
from our unpolished wooden floor.
The coffee machine brews in the kitchen.
I dance my way in the hallway of our young lives.
My wife, in bed, reading the latest article
on Patrick Chamoiseau, the laptop light
flickering on her glasses; she's determined
to complete her dissertation before any talk
of children.   I am mixing coffee,
cream, and sugar, tasting it,
searching for the right combination,
for that moment where just enough light
settles quietly in a corner,
when, as if by magic, we find ourselves
in the middle of the day. Suddenly,
my wife calls out from the bedroom,
Is the coffee ready yet?

Coming to Terms

After sleepless nights of re-reading student papers,
you've come to terms with assigning the final grades,
knowing full well that what you have is a glimpse,
a surface reading of a moment in someone's life,
someone you met three hours per week, a little over
two months; you also know that the students whose grades
you've agonized over are home with their families,
or traveling to some tiny island in the South Pacific
or that ancient land where Moses led his people
across the Red Sea, places that you only read about,
and what they want is the final product, that letter grade,
not the process. That morning, you stumble onto campus,
eyes squinting, but for the first time in a long time, you hear
the birds chirping, a spring song of love and kindness,
and you're feeling deep-deep joy, the old blood returning
when suddenly, a question from a corner of the office,
"Can I help you?" and before you have time, an answer
from the questioner, "If you are unhappy with your grade,
please send your complaint directly to your professor."
The old joy leaving, you are tired and dried,
as you explain in your now heavily-accented English
that you're simply here to submit grades.

You are thirty five, black hair, face round
like the moon; you are still mistaken for a student.
You wonder what students think when you,
unmistakably Asian, perpetually foreign,
economically uncertain, set foot in their English
classes. You know how you are feeling.

The Storm

I was at work when it hit:
a simple downpour, yet mysterious
somehow, waking us to an old world
where our ancestors, tadpoles
swam in the murky bottom.

My wife called. "The storm
took out the electricity.
Verizon said that they can't send
someone over 'til next Monday."
There was silence on both ends.

Over the years, she had learned to live
with my towels all over the place.
Over the years, I had accepted how
she organized our lives with a daily planner.

Quickly as it started, the storm left us.
We'd made it through the big stuff:
cultural differences, dissertation
defenses, tenure reviews,

but this—
A weekend together,
really together, where we eat
across the table from one another,
conversing about this or that
as if we were on our first date?

God help us.

Mooring

A twig breaks in half,
and against itself, a bough snaps.

On the horizon, a ship floats
in the stillness of dusk.

For months now, I've been up
at four in the morning.

I look at my wife sleeping,
a corner of her mouth twitches,

As the night is about to break.

No matter what happens,
I have you.

The Day My Worst Fear Came True

The restaurant was unremarkable,
hidden between a coffee shop and a Vietnamese
noodle place, within walking distance of
Portland State University. Our waitress
came over, filled our empty glasses,
a small Siam elephant tattooed on her right wrist,
and introduced herself as "Jennifer"
before leaving us to our menus.
Seeing a dish of papaya salad on a table
next to ours, I whispered to my wife,
"It's been a long time since I had Thai food."
When Jennifer returned,
I asked for beef in *Mussaman* curry
and chicken *Pad Ga Prau.*
I knew I couldn't finish both dishes, but I was greedy.
With a smile, I told the waitress to make it hot, extra spicy,
pointing to the four chilies icon on the menu.
"Are you sure?" She looked concerned.
"It's very spicy. Have you guys been here before?"
We shook our heads.
"We recommend to our new customers medium hot:
two chilies max."
Having been to Thai restaurants on the East Coast,
I smiled, "I'm Asian. I grew up eating this type of food.
I think I can handle it."

Jennifer went to the kitchen to place our order.
I thought the matter was settled, when minutes later,
Jennifer and a gentleman in khaki pants and blue shirt
emerged from the kitchen. "Sir, the 'four chilies' is very spicy.
Are you sure you want it that hot? We usually advise
our guests to try the medium hot first."
Slightly offended, I smiled: "Fine. Let's compromise.
Give me the three chilies, please. Thank you."
Waiting for my food, I thought to myself.
Maybe this food will transport me back home,

to grandfather praising grandmother
for her fine cooking, an unusual gesture in our family.
When the food came, I was not disappointed.
The aroma of beef cooked tenderly in peanut sauce,
with potatoes, onion, carrots, and bell peppers,
reminded me of the beef curry at my family's home
during New Year and Ancestors Day.
The minced chicken with basil, chilies, and
lemongrass made the meat both sweet and spicy.
Heck, even my wife's vegetarian pad Thai was delicious!
I took a bite of the beef in Mussaman curry,
and tears began filling my eyes.
Soon enough, my nose was running, and my hair,
drenched with sweat, stuck to my forehead.
Concerned, Jennifer came over to our table and refilled
my water glass. I avoided her eyes.
As I continued to eat, nose dripping
and eyes watery, my wife didn't know
whether she should help me or ridicule me.
With ears ringing, I looked up and saw, once again,
Jennifer refilling my water glass.
My wife suggested that maybe
we should take the leftovers back to the hotel.
As firmly as I could, I said "No,"
and asked, "Isn't it enough that I suffer
such humiliation within the confines
of this restaurant? I don't want
to be walking on the streets of Portland
announcing to the Pacific world
that I have lost my Khmer tongue."
I blew my nose into the napkin.

The Photographer and the Poet

(for Carol and Jim McCord)

The photographer and the poet are in the woods
behind their home, cherishing winter's gifts—
a red-bellied trout chasing sunlight in mid-air
over a shimmering stream, then the splash,
so familiar, comforting and humbling.

Suddenly, the wild & endless chirping
of birds was everywhere and nowhere.
The husband points in the direction
of a lone northern mockingbird bouncing
on the hard brown soil.

At home, the husband studies the photograph
his wife took, and composes a poem.
The pair has been chasing
the Divine Presence for years.

How They Stay with You

(after Gary Snyder's "Axe Handles")

The other day, my students and I were talking
about Maxine Hong Kingston and her talk story,
about the forces that shaped the writer—
stories, parents, ancestors,
incidents, dreams, and fate,
when I couldn't help myself.
I told them about Harry Marten,
whose office was adjacent to mine,
who would tell me stories
about his early years of teaching.
I drank them like coffee.
Then I told them about Jim McCord
who would get up at dawn
and scribble his poems,
drawing connections between his
breathing in and the chirpings outside.
I proudly said, "I too get up early to write."

And so it goes with influences.
It's in our stories, our teaching, our very being.
Tim O'Brien once said that stories are forever.
He must have known people like Harry and Jim.
They have a funny way of staying with you,
as you stand in front of the classroom
with faces staring back at you
and, right there and then, you know
you are part of something wonderful.

The Pavilion Dream

1.

In this recurring dream, I am with my family
at a pavilion on North Shore Drive, the side where water
meets land. People are watching my uncles and aunts fish.
In another version, my cousins and their children
are swimming, with sharks circling, and me screaming
at them to get out of the water, but they pay me no attention.
In the third, they are swimming, no sharks this time,
but the waves are ten feet high, smashing swimmers
against the pavilion's concrete wall, and again,
my cousins are not listening to me.

In these dreams, my family goes about their way.
My uncles and aunts laugh at a joke
that uses an old Khmer pun; my cousins and their children
laugh and play in the salty water.
I remember the sensations of the past
running through my waking body,
then the panic after the truth of such a dream settles,
the realization so deep, it hurts—
I am always the outsider peering in.

2.

On the morning after another version of this dream,
my wife told me that, while sleeping, I yelled out,
"I forget my Khmer. Oh no, I forget my Khmer."

"You were tossing and turning, then you turned quiet.
I got so nervous I shook you until you told me
to cut it out. Do you remember any of this?"

I tried to recollect that dream where I lost
my mother tongue, but before anything could happen,
my body tensed, my heart ached, a fist-sized stone

Sat heavily in my stomach.

An Invitation

(After Margrave's "Any Resemblance of Persons Living or Dead
Is Purely Coincidental")

My wife doesn't like it when I write about her.
Like in that poem about fireworks,
where she is made to look foolish,
her words, "a Western idiot who knows
nothing about the world."
Or, the one about our walk where I plant
a kiss, a butterfly kiss, on her cheek,
as we talk about the things that matter.
Or, the one about her addiction to coffee,
which is simply not true. I'm the addict.

At my readings, she has to sit through
the crap I tell strangers and friends.
I don't know which is worse: to have strangers
or friends know about our private world.
 "It doesn't matter," she says. "I don't like it one bit.
The issue here is my privacy."
I respond, "It's my life too. And you are part of that."

I, then, go on an unnecessary tirade
on freedom of expression and censorship,
on the artist's role in creating order
in the chaos that is life, or some shit like that.
I then say, "Consider this an invitation
for you to write. To tell your side of our stories."
She retorts, "Wait! Don't you have to be famous *first?*"

VII: CAMBODIA

The Case is Closed

He calls every other weekend.
Panic in his voice, his heart racing.
"Two in the morning, I woke up sweating,
out of breath." His voice's shaking.
He talks of losing his house, wife, and daughter.
Everyone tells him that it's a matter of protocol,
that it is not personal, that the car insurance
will take care of everything.

He says, "This is not me. I'm now a stranger
to myself. I know that things will be fine,
but I cannot control these thoughts.
The doctor told me to close my eyes and relax.
'Just imagine the ocean,' he said.
Imagine me sitting there and thinking of the ocean!
You remember what happened?
We were on a boat leaving Thailand;
everyone was crying and vomiting.
I got sick just thinking about it.

Then the doctor said to imagine being in nature,
to think of the cool shade that the trees make.
When the Khmer Rouge moved us, I was separated
from my brigade. I found myself in the forest,
all alone, and I discovered those bodies—
tied and blindfolded, torn and darkly mangled.
The doctor then told me to imagine a quiet lake.
But I don't like any lakes around here.
They're not like the ones in Cambodia."

A gulf of silence settles between us.

I too remind him that a settlement was reached.
"You got that letter from the lawyer weeks ago.
You held it in your hands. It's over now.
Your case is closed."

"I know that," he says. "Everybody's been saying it,
so it must be true. But I don't know why I still can't sleep.
I got crazy when that summons came in the mail.
Everything went out of control, like it was Cambodia
all over again, where we were told to relocate every few months.
After a while, you forgot what home felt like,
and you didn't know if you parents were alive,
and you didn't know where your sisters were.
You were completely alone;
you were at the mercy of the state.
I know, as you say, 'It's official.
The case is closed. It's over.'
Yes, everything is over now."

Inheritance

My uncles, aunts, and grandmother all agree:
It was a difficult time. People starving.
You don't trust the children. You don't trust
your neighbors, friends, even your family.
But this can't be. It must be something I read.
Something I taught, pointed out in a lecture,
maybe discovered in a conversation with a survivor,
a man with ashen hair and toothless smile,
in an apartment complex in Lowell, MA.

Anyway, these are the images I carry with me:
rib-cage thin. Diarrhea. Chicken blindness. Dysentery.
Hands tied behind your back, legs too weak to crawl, eyes bulging,
white with petrifaction, irises black as night, wings broken,
spirit destroyed, only paranoia and hunger ruled the day
and the night, my mother's body, difficulty with breathing,
bones sharp as knives, eternal loneliness, eternal sadness,
the sour taste of tamarind, Mother dead from starvation,
her sister, a branch in hand, sharpened by hunger,
hunting for lizards, snakes, crickets, for dark green leaves,
all black—black pajamas, black hair, black sadness,
always night, always cold, cold wind and loneliness,
fear of whispering wind and unseen eyes, pineapple eyes,
everywhere and nowhere, strangers, friends, family
disappearing, without struggle, without a sound,
the only evidence is the fear in those trembling,
working the fields, lips so dry it hurts when it rains,
the corpses strewn about as if for a group pose,
in a ditch along the dirt road, plastic bag wrapped
around the heads, a statement on the value
of human life, unworthy of a single bullet.

Their motto: to kill you is no loss, but what is
lost is family, the old way of life, being human,
and what is gained is a new world order,
monks disrobed, temples destroyed, elders useless,

109

the new temple is a pyramid of human skulls,
where a boy, illiterate and verging on puberty,
dressed in black pajamas, an AK-47 on his back,
a *kromar* around his neck, guards the entrance,
his old family gone, his new family is the organization,
his new mother is hate, his new father is Angka,
to which everything must be reported, Angka,
the figurehead, the godhead, the master of the universe,
from which, to which, everything revolves, the giver
and taker of life, human or otherwise, the maker of reality.

Lucky

(for Harry and Ginit Marten)

Before I tasted sadness, Mother passed away.
Before Father had other children, I left for the States.
In third grade, I carved my name in English,
polished smooth, straight, full of pumpkin seeds,
while my half-brothers toiled under Cambodia's hot sun.
In high school, I whimpered in the principal's office
for skipping classes and forging grandmother's name,
while one of my brothers was hung upside down,
kicked by the Thai police for working without papers.
I avoided the gang life because where we were,
back then, there wasn't enough of us to be a gang.
After high school, I made way across the States
and, for ten years, hung around the great columns
of Long Beach City College, in search of ghosts
that spoke my tongue, where I tasted isolation
and called it muse, only to find, of all people,
Bukowski, that patron saint of the dispossessed,
now a literary god for hipsters, Sean Penn, and Bono.
In graduate school, I found a wife and a friend.
In one of the worst markets in years, I was offered a job
to teach at a private college in the East Coast, me
—the guy who played hooky and failed Home Ec.—
and the guy who hired me, the one who can dismantle
an A-bomb with just his words, taught me
how to teach, read, write, and ask good questions,
to listen to the unsaid things that people say,
to move tidal waves with humor and grace.
I have much to learn, friends, but this I know,
I have always counted myself lucky, but never *this* lucky.

Fragments

I

The night sky lit like fireworks,
the air smells of burnt skin.
Mothers cry for children.
The boy clutches his grandmother's body.
Bodies fall,
pieces of someone—
a neighbor, a friend,
an aunt, maybe.

The boy asks,
"Where is Mother?"

The jungle is silent.
The earth stands still.

II

The boy awakens
from a nightmare.

The bomb, a firebird,
spreads its wings.

The boy is panting,
sweat dampens the earth.

Somewhere in this mist and fog,
outside the UN refugee camp,
a woman howls.

And the boy
thinks about his mother.

III

In our apartment, in Upstate New York,
we watch fireworks from our living room window.
The college where we teach is celebrating—

aging alumni and retired professors
gather under the boom.

I sit back on the futon
trying to rest, eyes closed, sweating.

My fiancée looks out the window,
"There's something about fireworks,"
she says to me. "Something
about them that appeals to everyone."

Khao-I-Dang Refugee Camp (1980)

A hot, dusty, endless stretch of dry earth.
Early mornings, my uncles and aunts disappeared
into the red-brown haze. I'd roam, branch in hand
looking for crickets and lizards in the dirt field,
where on weekends young men enacted
centuries-old bloody conflicts between
Viet Nam and Cambodia with a soccer ball.

On this field I saw the crucifixion of Christ.
A mesmerizing horror show, presented by the most gentle
of people, our friends and teachers, whose Church groups
would send our family to Boston, Philadelphia, and St. Cloud,
places as foreign to us as snow, Christmas, and birthdays.
I found the film difficult to watch as the dust clogged
my young lungs. Was this the America we were heading to?

That evening I found Grandmother tending
the bruises on her oldest living son, caught
by the Thai police for night fishing
to supplement the meager food ration for our family.

Goodbye, Cambodia

The panic on men's faces,
their hands over their heads,
as they prayed to Lord Buddha.
The running and yelling,
the children shrieking, mothers crying,
the stench of vomit and urine.

Somehow, I found myself on deck
waves smashing against the boat,
when a woman with long black hair
smiled from afar then seconds later,
dove headfirst into the water. In a flash,
I saw her fishtail flap,
a gentle, simple splash.

That night I slept on Grandma's lap,
feeling assured that I need not worry,
my mother, the mermaid, Cambodia,
will always be with me.

In Pol Pot's Shadow

A man outside in his orange sarong
talking with the police then arguing
over his right to beat and rape his wife,
ran into his home and promised the police
to butcher them with a kitchen knife.

The officers ran to their patrol cars
and radioed for backup. Minutes later,
an ambulance, and at least five patrol cars
and a helicopter surrounded the brown house.
The officers went in with their shotguns
and came out carrying the man whose arms
and legs were tied. We, his neighbors,
fellow refugees ourselves, stood under
the elm tree, in Pol Pot's shadow.

On the Porch with Grandma

The other day Grandma and I were sitting
on the front porch on the futon swing.

It was early morning, the summer heat
had yet to arrive. We were just watching

the cars drive by when I noticed a butterfly
flashing its bright-yellow orange

near a row of flowers at the entrance.
There in the air, I pointed in its direction.

Grandma's eyes followed, as I uttered
in broken Khmer, "See that flying thing!

That little bird. What do you call it,
That little bird with colorful wings?"

The Importance of Names

What is this I hear about you wanting to be called
by someone else's name?
Your cousin told me the other day.
Let me tell you how you got the name you have.
When you were born, relatives from afar,
from the four directions of the earth,
came on foot to our tiny village
in Battambang.
They came to see you:
their nephew, cousin, and grandson.
Some brought fresh fruit,
others mangoes, figs, and dried meat.
They were mostly farmers.
Your father's mother, your other grandmother
came all the way from the East,
now in Viet Nam's territory.
Her teeth were black
from betel nut, and she told me,
"I crossed mountains and rivers
to see my grandson."
We decided then to call you
"Joum"
because everyone gathered around.
The relatives greeted each other,
some for the first time,
others asked about this cousin or that aunt,
and everyone was happy
until you cried.
You cried and cried incessantly; it was so bad
that nobody wanted to be around you.
I slept by your side
to let your poor mother rest,
then we took you to see the village shaman,
who declared that your spirit mother
missed you and wanted you back.
If you were to stay in our world,

we had to have a naming ceremony
where you would be given a new name
so that your spirit mother could not find
you.
That is how you, my grandson, got your name:
"Kong."
It's a name befitting a child who survives.
You have to live up to it.
You have to endure.

My Uncle

got up at 5, drove
his wife to work, dropped
his sister and brother-in-law
at the train station, took
his children to school, returned
home to have breakfast.

He ate gruel with salted
fish as if he had just
escaped from the Khmer Rouge;
after three years, eight months,
and twenty days of hard labor,
rice and water never tasted better.

He drank hot jasmine tea with
the TV news blasting, paying attention
to words like "crimes," "human rights
abuses," "tribunal," "prosecution," looking
up "indictment," "custody" in his Huffman-
and-Proum English-Khmer dictionary.

By 9 a.m., my uncle unlocked the deadbolt
to his store, picked the videos
from the return box, cleared them
in his computer, and when the bell rang,
he looked up smiling, "Good morning.
Welcome to King Videos,"
as if he were the luckiest man alive.

Beginnings

(for Paul)

1.
The Viet Nam War, a dragon that breathed in the morning air
and spat out orange mist, drowned rice paddies and uprooted palm trees,
forcing a young man and his uncle to leave his farming village
on Cambodia's southern border to escape conscription.
The man and his uncle shaved their heads, dressed in yellow robes,
and begged alms from their countrymen, arriving on the other side,
in Battambang, where they met another farming family.
The young man took a liking to the oldest daughter
while the uncle eyed the girl's aunt.
So it came about: the nephew married the niece,
the uncle wedded the aunt, and on the birth
of the young couple's first and only son,
relatives from east and west came
to celebrate what would be their last celebration
before another war took everything.

2.
In that same year, miles away in Easton, PA,
a young man's draft notice arrived in a plain white envelope.
His hand felt the creased seal, his heart trembling
with vision of Nam. Earlier that year, his mother had a dream
that came true: the wounding of his two older brothers.
Now his mother dreamed: he was killed in combat.
Driven by love, she wrote to her senator, requesting
an exemption for her youngest son.
So it came about: the young man was sent
to Arizona, working as a MP officer protecting
America's desert and secret military base.
Upon his return, he reunited
with his high school sweetheart, and the couple
had two children, a boy and a girl.

3.
Decades later at a university, the first and only son said
to the girl in the graduate student office,
"I'm not good at talking to people. If you don't mind,
I prefer to work on my dissertation."
For reasons unknown to him, he can't stop himself
from talking to her.
Now they are married, teaching at a small college
in Upstate New York, with him chattering away.

4.
Listen, did the stars align in their rightful places
and the moon shine just for them?
What force pulled all these couples together?
What moved them: war, a parent's love,
invisible hands?

Gruel

We were talking about survival
when my uncle told me this.
"When you were young,
we had nothing to eat.
Your grandmother saved for you
the thickest part of her rice gruel.
Tasting that cloudy mixture of salt,
water, and grain, you cried out,
'This is better than beef curry.'"

All my life I told myself I never knew
suffering under the regime, only love.
This is still true.

Acknowledgments

Earlier versions of some poems have appeared or forthcoming in the following journals, *The New York Quarterly; Numéro Cinq; The Journal of War, Literature, and the Arts; Misfit; The Más Tequila Review; Cadence Collective; Silver Birch Press; NYADP Journal;* and anthologies; *Transnational Cambodia: Cambodians Writing across Continents; With Our Eyes Wide Open: Poems of the New American Century;* and *Two-Countries: Daughters and Sons of Immigrant Parents.*

Without the love and support of friends and family, this book would not be possible. I'm forever grateful to them, especially Yoeum Preng, Bunyonn Tuon, Nicole Calandra, Tony Gloeggler, Clint Margrave, Harry and Ginit Marten, Jim and Carol McCord, Jordan Smith, April Selley, Floyd Cheung, Teri Yamada, Alan Catlin, my colleagues in the English Department at Union College, and fellow poets from the Schenectady and Murray groups.

I am especially grateful to Raymond Hammond who, upon the recommendation of Tony Gloeggler, gave me this wonderful opportunity to share my stories with the world. I am honored to be a part of the NYQ poet community.

CPSIA information can be obtained
at www.ICGtesting.com
Printed in the USA
FSOW01n0745260817
37961FS